Babel Books, Inc.

 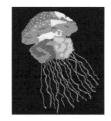 

Children's Illustrated Modern

English-Italian
Italian-English

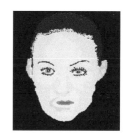

Dictionary

By: Yoselem G. Divincenzo

Compiled ,Translated and Illustrated by :

Yoselem G. Divincenzo

Copyright © 2008 by Yoselem G. Divincenzo

1st Edition

ISBN 978-0-9800127-2-9

Printed in the United States

For information, address:

Babel Books, Inc.

93-64 204th St.

Hollis, NY 11423

Website: www.babelbooks.us

Introduction

Children's Illustrated Modern English-Italian/Italian-English Dictionary was created based on the necessity that every child needs to build self confidence and motivation on the critical years of kindergarten to third grade; as well for adults learning English or Italian as a second language.

The words utilized were carefully selected to fit into the age-appropriateness. It summarizes how to successfully learn the new language introducing the idea of alphabetical order to be prepared for a higher-level dictionary; containing a variety of everyday words with colorful illustrations that will help children develop interest in letter, sounds, reading and writing. The new colorful art illustrations will bring words to life making the learning process interesting and entertaining.

Introduzione

Dizionario Moderno Illustrato Di Inglese-Italiano/Italiano-Inglese Dei Bambini è stato generato ha basato sulla necessità di che ogni bambino ha bisogno per sviluppare l'auto sicurezza e la motivazione sugli anni critici dell'asilo al terzo grado; pure per imparare degli adulti inglese o italiano come seconda lingua.

Le parole utilizzate sono state selezionate con attenzione per inserire nella età-convenienza. Ricapitola come imparare con successo la nuova lingua che introduce l'idea di ordine alfabetico essere preparato per un dizionario di più alto livello; contenendo una varietà di parole giornalieri con le illustrazioni vivacemente colorato che per aiutare i bambini a sviluppare interesse nella lettera, nei suoni, nella lettura e nella scrittura. Le nuove illustrazioni vivacemente colorato di arte porteranno le parole a vita che fa l'apprendimento che interessa e che intrattiene.

Contents:

Italian Pronunciation

a ah as in English "apple"

b b as in English in "bed"

c k before "a, o, or u"; ch before "e or I"

d d as in English "doll"

e eh as in English "pen"

f f as in English "farm"

g g before "a or u" as "garden", j before "e or i" "jam"

h always silent

i ee as in English "feed"

j j as in English "jazz"

k k as in English "kite"

l l as in English "lamb"

m m as in English "man"

n n as in English "name"

o o as in English "cone"

p as in English "pie"

q k as in English "kite"

r r as in English "rat"

s s as in English "sad"

t t as in in the name "Tom"

u oo as in English "moon"

v v as in English "vest"

w w as in English "wagon"

y ee as an English in "need"

z ts so the English word pizza is "peetsah"

Pronuncia Inglese

a come "a" in Italiano "angelo"

b come la "b" in Italiano "banbino"

c come la "c" in Italiano "camera"

ch come la "c" dolce in Italiano "cena"

d come la "d" in Italiano "dado"

e como la "e" simple in Italiano "caffè"

f como la "f" in Italiano "fiore"

g come la "g" dura in Italiano "gola"

h come la "h" in Italiano "hotel" " (espirando aira con la gola)

i come la "i" in Italiano " india"

j come la "g" dolce in Italiano " gelo"

k come la "k" dura in Italiano "casa"

l come la "l" in Italiano " lama"

m come la "m" in Italiano " madre"

n come la "n" in Italiano "nave"

o come la "o" in Italiano " orso"

p como la "p" in Italiano " palma"

q come la "q" in Italiano " quadro"

r come la "r" in Italiano " radio"

s come la "s" in Italiano " salsiccia"

t come la "t" in Italiano " torta"

u come la "u" in Italiano "uva"

v come la "v" in Italiano " vespa"

w come la "uo" in Italiano " uova"

y come la "i" in Italiano " iota"

z z as come la "s" in Italiano " rosa"

4

A

airplane *(eir-plein)*
aeroplano *(ah-eh-roh-plah-noh)*

alligator *(a-li-ghei-ror)*
coccodrillo *(coh-coh-dree-loh)*

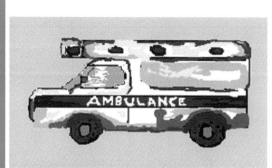

ambulance *(am-biu-lans)*
ambulanza *(ahm-boo-lahn-zah)*

angel
(ein-shol)

angelo *(ahn-sheh-loh)*

ant
(ant)

formica *(fohr-mee-cah)*

apartment
(a-part-ment)

appartamento *(ah-pahr-tah-mehn-toh)*

apple
(a-pol)

mela *(meh-lah)*

aquarium
(ah-cue-rium)

acquario *(ah-coo-ah-ree-oh)*

5

A

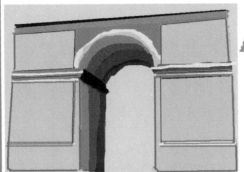

arc *(arc)*   arco *(ahr-coh)*

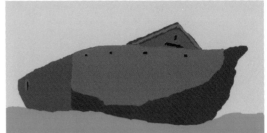

ark *(ark)*   arca *(ahr-cah)*

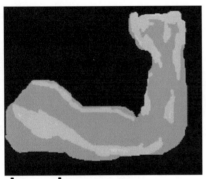

arm *(arm)*

braccio *(brah-choh)*

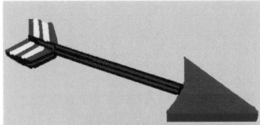

arrow *(e-rrou)*

freccia *(freh-chah)*

athlete *(a-tli)*

atleta *(ah-tleh-tah)*

automobile *(au-ro-mo-bil)*
automobile *(ah-oo-toh-moh-bee-leh)*

autumn *(o-rom)*

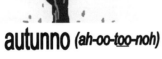

autunno *(ah-oo-too-noh)*

award *(a-word)*

premio *(preh-mee-oh)*

6

B

baby *(bei-bi)*
bambino *(bahm-bee-noh)*

backpack
(bhak-pak)

zaino
(zah-ee-noh)

bag
(bhag)

sacchetto *(sah-keh-toh)*

ballet
(ba-let)

balletto
(bah-leh-toh)

balloon *(ba-lun)*
aerostato *(ah-eh-rohs-tah-toh)*

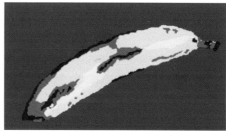

banana
(ba-na-na)

banana
(bah-nah-nah)

bandage *(ban-dehsh)*
fascia *(fah-shah)*

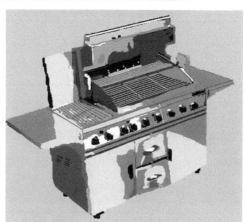

barbecue *(bar-bi-kiu)*
grigliata *(greeh-glee-ah-tah)*

7

B

barn *(barn)*
granaio *(grah-nah-ee-oh)*

basket *(bas-quet)*

cestino *(chehs-tee-noh)*

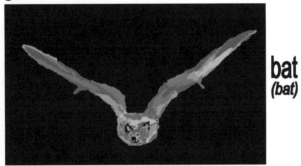

bat *(bat)*

pipistrello *(pee-pee-strah-loh)*

battery *(ba-re-ri)*

batteria *(bah-teh-ree-ah)*

bear *(behr)*   orso *(ohr-soh)*

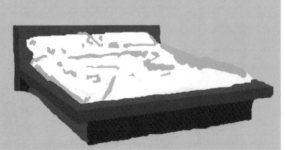

bed *(bed)*   letto *(leh-toh)*

bee *(bii)*

ape *(ah-peh)*

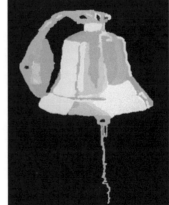

bell *(bel)*

campana *(cahm-pah-nah)*

B

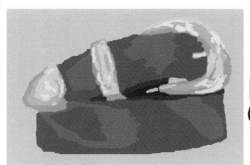

belt *(belt)*

cintola *(seen-toh-lah)*

bench *(bensh)*   banco *(bahn-coh)*

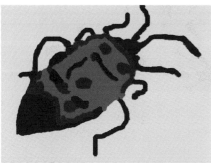

beetle *(bi-rol)*

scarabeo *(s-cah-rah-beh-oh)*

bicycle *(bai-si-col)*
bicicletta *(bee-chee-cleh-tah)*

binoculars *(bai-no-kiu-lars)*

binocolo *(bee-noh-coh-loh)*

bird *(berd)*

uccello *(oo-cheh-loh)*

biscuit *(bis-ket)*

biscotto *(bees-coh-toh)*

bison *(bai-son)*

bisonte *(bee-sohn-teh)*

9

blackberry *(blak-beh-rri)*
mora *(moh-rah)*

blacksmith *(blak-smeth)*
maniscalco *(mah-nees-cahl-coh)*

boat *(bout)*
barca *(bar-cahh)*

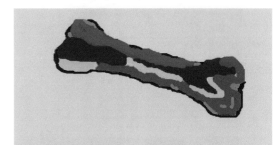

bone *(boh-un)*   **osso** *(oh-soh)*

book
(buk)

libro
(lee-broh)

boot
(buht)

stivale
(s-tee-vah-leh)

bottle
(ba-rol)

bottiglia
(boo-teeg-lee-ah)

bouquet
(buh-keh)

bouquet
(boo-keh)

B

bowl *(bo-hul)* ciotola *(shoh-toh-lah)*

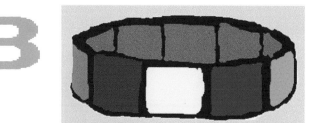

bracelet *(breis-let)*
braccialetto *(brah-chah-leh-toh)*

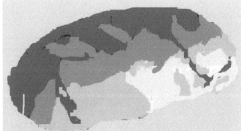

bread *(bred)*   pane *(pah-neh)*

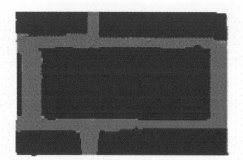

bricks *(briks)*

mattoni *(mah-toh-nee)*

broccoli *(bro-co-li)*

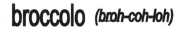

broccolo *(broh-coh-loh)*

broom *(brum)*

scopa *(s-coh-pah)*

bucket *(ba-ket)*

secchio *(seh-kee-oh)*

bulb *(bolb)*

ornamento *(ohr-nah-mehn-toh)*   11

burglar
(behr-glehr)

svaligiatore
(s-vah-lee-shah-toh-reh)

bus *(bas)*   **autobus** *(ah-oo-toh-boos)*

butter
(ba-ter)

burro *(boo-rroh)*

butterfly
(ba-rer-flai)

farfalla
(fahr-fah-llah)

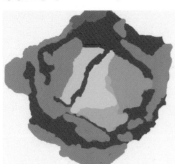

cabbage
(ca-besh)

cavolo *(cah-voh-loh)*

cabinet
(ca-bi-net)

armadietto *(ahr-mah-dee-eh-toh)*

cactus
(cakts)

cactus
(cahc-toos)

cage
(keish)

gabbia
(gah-bee-ah)

12

cake
(keik)

torta
(tohr-tah)

calf
(caf)

vitello
(vee-teh-loh)

camel *(que-mol)* **camello** *(cah-meh-loh)*

camera
(ca-meh-ra)

macchina fotografica
(mah-kee-nah/pho-toh-grah-phi-cah)

can
(ken)

barattolo
(bah-rah-toh-loh)

canary
(ke-ne-ri)

canarino
(cah-nah-ree-noh)

candle
(ken-dol)

candela
(cahn-deh-lah)

candy
(Jken-di)

dolciumi *(dool-choo-mee)*

canoe *(ca-nu)*   **canoa** *(cah-noh-ah)*

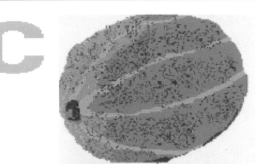

cantaloupe *(ken-ta-lop)*
melone *(meh-loh-neh)*

carnation *(car-nei-shion)*
garofano *(gah-roh-pha-noh)*

carpet
(car-pet)

moquette
(moh-keht)

carrot *(ke-rrot)*
carota *(cah-roh-tah)*

castle
(ca-sol)

castello
(cahs-teh-loh)

cat
(cat)

gatto
(gah-toh)

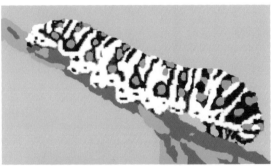

caterpillar *(ca-rer-pi-ler)*
bruco *(broo-coh)*

chair
(cer)

sedia
(seh-dee-ah)

cheese
(ciss)

formaggio
(fohr-mah-shoh)

cheetah *(chi-ra)* **ghepardo** *(geh-pahr-doh)*

cherry
(che-ri)

ciliegia
(chee-lee-eh-sha)

chess *(cess)* **scacchi** *(s-kah-kee)*

chicken *(ci-ken)* **pollo** *(poo-loh)*

chimney
(cim-ni)

ciminiera *(chee-mee-nee-eh-rah)*

chimpanzee
(cim-pan-si)

scimpanzè *(sheem-pahn-zeh)*

15

C

chocolate *(cioh-co-leit)*
cioccolata *(shoh-coh-lah-tah)*

church *(ciohrsh)*

chiesa *(quee-eh-sah)*

circus *(sir-cus)*

circo *(sheer-coh)*

clock *(clock)*

orologio *(ohr-loh-shoh)*

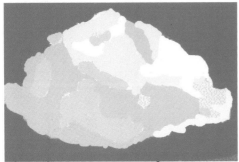

cloud *(claud)* **nuvola** *(noo-voh-lah)*

clown *(claun)*

pagliaccio *(pahg-lee-ah-choh)*

cobweb *(cob-web)*

ragnatela *(rahg-nee-ah-teh-lah)*

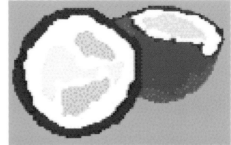

coconut *(co-co-not)* **cocco** *(coh-coh)*

16

comb
(khaomb)

pettine
(peh-tee-neh)

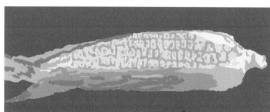

corn *(corn)*   mais *(mah-eez)*

cowboy
(cau-boi)

cowboy
(cah-oo-boh-ee)

cow *(cau)*   vacca *(vah-cah)*

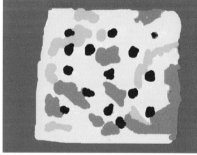

cracker
(cra-ker)

galleta
(gah-lleh-tah)

crab *(crab)*   granchio *(grahn-kee-oh)*

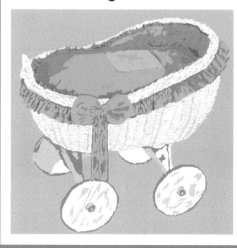

crib
(crib)

culla
(coo-lah)

crocodile *(cro-ca-drol)*
cocodrillo *(coh-coh-dree-loh)*

17

C

cross *(cross)* **croce** *(croh-cheh)*

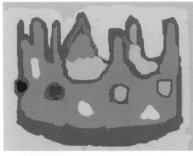

crown *(craun)*

corona *(coh-roh-nah)*

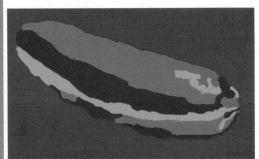

cucumber *(kiu-cum-ber)*
cetriolo *(ceh-tree-oh-loh)*

cup *(cap)*

tazza *(tah-zzah)*

D

daisy *(dei-si)*

margherita *(mahr-geh-ree-tah)*

deer *(dii-ehr)* **cervo** *(chehr-voh)*

desk *(desk)*

scrittorio *(s-cree-toh-ree-oh))*

dice *(dais)*

dado *(dah-doh)*

18

D

disk
(disk)

dischetto
(dees-keh-toh)

doctor
(doc-tor)

dottore
(doh-toh-reh)

dog
(dog)

cane
(cah-neh)

doll
(doll)

bambola
(bahm-boh-lah)

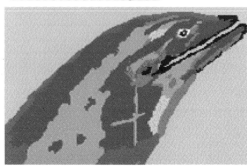

dolphin
(dol-fin)

delfino
(dehl-phee-noh)

domino *(do-mi-no)*
domino *(doh-mee-noh)*

donkey
(don-qui)

mulo *(moo-loh)*

door
(dohr)

porta
(pohr-tah)

19

D

dragon *(dra-gon)*   drago *(drah-goh)*

dress
(dress)

vestito   *(vehs-tee-toh)*

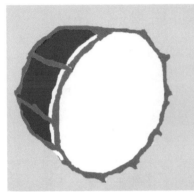

drum
(drom)

tamburo
(tahm-boo-roh)

duck
(dack)

anatra
(ah-nah-trah)

E

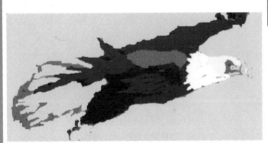

eagle *(i-gol)*   aquila *(ah-coo-ee-lah)*

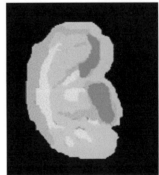

ear
(ii-er)

orecchio
(oh-rah-kee-oh)

earphone *(ir-fon)*
auricolari *(ah-oo-ree-coo-lah-ree)*

20

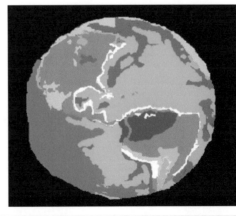

earth
(ert)

terra
(teh-rrah)

E

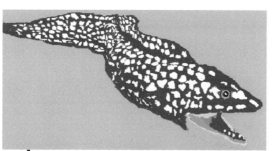

eel *(iiol)*   **anguilla** *(ahn-goo-ee-lah)*

egg *(egg)*   **uovo** *(oo-oh-voh)*

eggplant *(egg-plant)*
melanzana *(meh-lahn-zah-nah)*

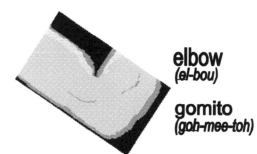

elbow
(el-bou)

gomito
(goh-mee-toh)

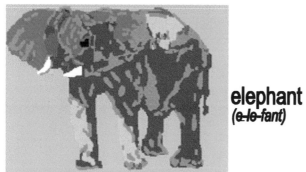

elephant
(e-le-fant)

elefante *(eh-leh-phan-teh)*

elevator
(eh-leh-vei-ror)

ascensore
(ahs-cehn-soh-reh)

elk *(elk)*   **alce** *(ahl-cheh)*

engineer
(en-shi-niir)

ingegnere *(een-sheh-nee-eh-reh)*

21

E

envelope *(en-ve-lop)*
busta *(boos-tah)*

escalator *(es-ca-leh-ii-ror)*
scala *(s-cah-lah)*

eskimo *(es-ki-mo)*
eschimese *(ehs-kee-meh-seh)*

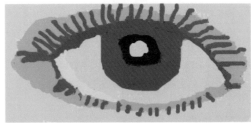

eye
(ai)

occhio
(oh-kee-oh)

F

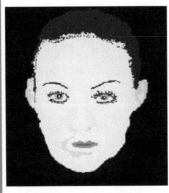

face
(feis)

faccia
(fah-chah)

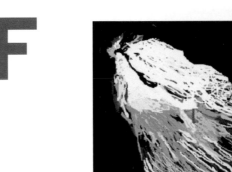

fairy
(fe-ri)

fata
(fah-tah)

falcon
(fal-con)

falcone
(fahl-coh-neh)

fan
(fen)

ventilatore *(vehn-tee-lah-toh-reh)*

F

farm *(farm)*   tenuta *(teh-noo-tah)*

acquaio *(ah-coo-ah-ee-oh)*

faucet
(fo-set)

feather
(feh-der)

piuma
(pee-oo-mah)

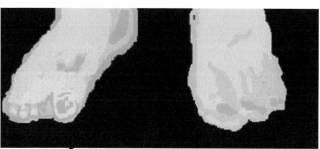

feet *(fiit)*   piedi *(pee-eh-dee)*

fence
(fens)

staccionata *(s-tah-choh-nah-tah)*

fern
(fern)

felce
(fehl-cheh)

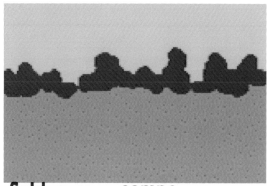

field *(fi-old)*   campo *(cahm-poh)*

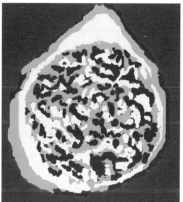

fig
(fig)

fico
(fee-coh)

23

F

finger *(fin-gher)*   dito *(dee-toh)*

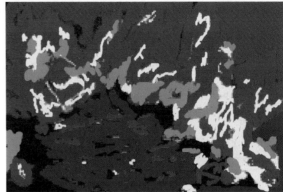

fire *(fa-ier)*   fuoco *(foo-oh-coh)*

fish *(fish)*   pesce *(peh-sheh)*

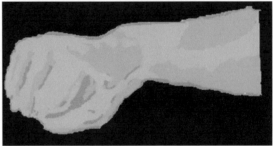

fist *(fist)*   pugno *(poog-nee-oh)*

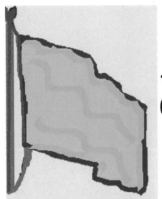

flag *(flahg)*

bandiera *(bahn-dee-eh-rah)*

flamingo *(fla-min-go)*

fiammingo *(fee-ah-meen-goh)*

flashlight *(flahsh-lait)*

lanterna *(lahn-tehr-nah)*

flower *(fla-uer)*

fiore *(fee-oh-reh)*

24

F

fly *(flai)*   mosca *(mohs-cah)*

forest
(fo-rest)

foresta
(foh-rehs-tah)

fork
(fork)

forchetta
(fohr-cheh-tah)

fox
(fox)

volpe
(vohl-peh)

frame *(freim)*   cornice *(cohr-nee-cheh)*

frog
(frog)

rana
(rah-nah)

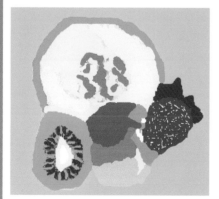

fruit *(frut)*   frutta *(froo-tah)*

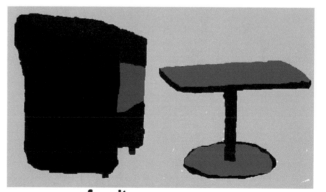

furniture *(for-ni-tur)*
mobile *(moh-bee-leh)*

25

G

garage *(ga-rash)*
postoauto *(pohs-toh-ah-oo-toh)*

garden *(gar-den)*   **giardino** *(shar-dee-noh)*

garlic
(gar-lic)

aglio
(ahg-lee-oh)

gate *(geit)*   **portone** *(pohr-toh-neh)*

gazelle *(ga-zel)* **gazzella** *(gah-zeh-lah)*

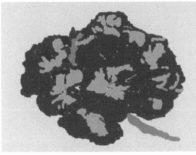

geranium
(sheh-re-nium)

geranio
(sheh-rah-nee-oh)

gift
(ghift)

regalo
(reh-gah-loh)

giraffe
(shi-raf)

giraffa
(she-rah-pha)

G

gladiolus
(gla-dio-los)

gladiolo
(glah-dee-oh-loh)

glasses
(gla-ses)

occhiali *(oh-kee-ah-lee)*

globe
(glob)

globo
(gloh-boh)

glove
(glouv)

guanto
(goo-ahn-toh)

goat *(gout)*   capra *(cah-prah)*

goblet
(ga-blet)

bicchiere
(bee-kee-ah-reh)

goose *(gus)*   oca *(oh-cah)*

grapes *(greips)*   uva *(oo-vah)*

27

G

grass *(grass)* prato *(prah-toh)*

grasshopper *(gra-sho-per)*
cavalletta *(cah-vah-leh-tah)*

guitar
(ghi-tar)

chitarra
(kee-tah-rrah)

gull
(goul)

gabbiano
(gah-bee-ah-noh)

H

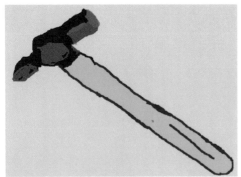

ham *(ham)* prosciutto *(proh-shoo-toh)*

hamburger *(ham-bur-gher)*
hamburger *(hahm-boor-gehr)*

hammer *(ha-mer)*
martello *(mahr-teh-loh)*

hammock *(ha-meck)*
amaca *(ah-mah-cah)*

28

H

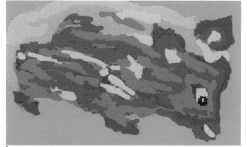

hamster *(hams-ter)*
porcellino *(pohr-cheh-lee-noh)*

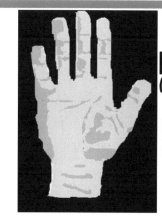

hand
(hand)

mano
(mah-noh)

handbag
(hand-bag)

borsetta
(bohr-seh-tah)

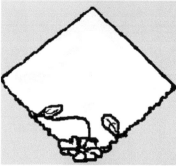

handkerchief
(hand-ker-kif)

fazzoletto
(fah-zoh-leh-toh)

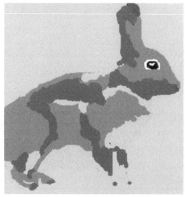

hare
(her)

lepre
(leh-preh)

harp
(harp)

arpa
(ahr-pah)

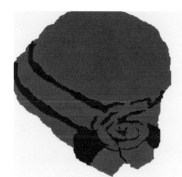

hat
(jat)

cappello *(cah-peh-lloh)*

hawk *(jak)*   **falco** *(fahl-coh)*

29

H

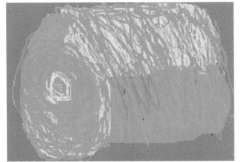

hay *(jey)*   fieno *(fee-eh-noh)*

head *(jed)*

testa *(tehs-tah)*

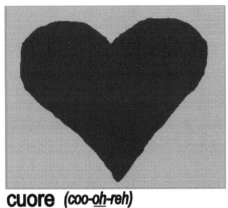

heart *(hart)*

cuore *(coo-oh-reh)*

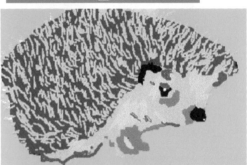

hedgehog *(hedsh-jog)*
porcospino *(pohr-cohs-pee-noh)*

helmet *(jel-met)*

casco *(cahs-coh)*

hen *(jen)*

gallina *(gah-lee-nah)*

highway *(jai-guei)*
autostrada *(ah-oo-tohs-trah-dah)*

hoe *(jou)*

zappa *(zah-pah)*

30

H

honey
(ja-ni)

miele
(mee-eh-leh)

hook
(juk)

gancio
(gahn-choh)

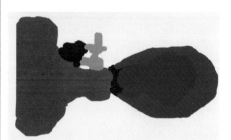

horn *(jom)* bocina *(boh-see-nah)*

horse
(jors)

cavallo
(cah-vah-loh)

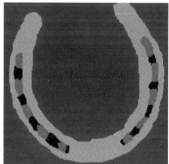

horseshoe
(jors-shu)

ferro di cavallo
(feh-rroh/dee/cah-vah-loh)

hourglass
(aur-glas)

clessidra
(cleh-see-drah)

house *(jous)*
casa *(cah-sah)*

hydrant
(jai-drant)

idrante
(ee-drahn-teh)

31

ice cream
(ais/crim)

gelato
(sheh-lah-toh)

ice cubes
(ais/kiubs)

cubetti di ghiaccio
(coo-beh-tee/deh/gee-ah-choh)

ice skates
(ais-skeits)

pattini da ghiaccio
(pah-tee-nee/dah/gee-ah-choh)

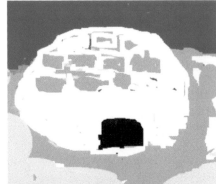

igloo
(ai-glu)

igloo
(ee-gloo)

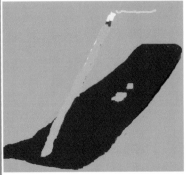

incense
(in-sens)

incenso
(een-shehn-soh)

iris
(ai-ris)

iris
(ee-rees)

iron
(ai-ron)

stirare   *(s-tee-rah-reh)*

island *(ai-land)*   **isola** *(ee-soh-lah)*

J

jack in the box
(shack/in/de/box)

scatola sorpresa
(s-cah-toh-lah/sohr-preh-sah)

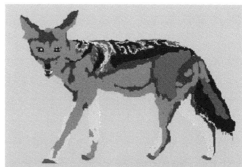

jackal *(sha-kol)*   **sciacallo** *(shah-cah-loh)*

jacket
(shah-ket)

giacchetta
(shah-keh-tah)

jaguar *(sha-guar)*
giaguaro *(shah-goo-ah-roh)*

jail
(sheil)

carcere
(cahr-ceh-reh)

jam
(sham)

marmellata
(mehr-meh-lah-tah)

jar
(shar)

vasetto
(vah-seh-toh)

jasmine
(shahs-meen)

gelsomino *(shehl-soh-mee-noh)*

33

J

jeans
(shins)

jeans
(sheens)

jelly beans
(sheh-li/bins)

caramella alla frutta
(cah-rah-meh-lah/ah-lah/froo-tah)

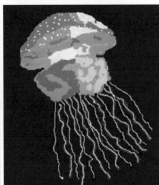

jelly fish
(sheh-li/fish)

medusa
(meh-doo-sah)

jig-saw puzzle
(shig/sau/pa-zol)

puzzle
(pah-zohl)

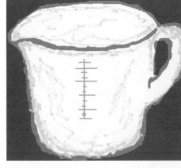

jug
(shog)

brocca
(broh-cah)

jockey
(sho-ki)

jockey
(hoh-kee)

juice
(shuss)

succo
(soo-coh)

jungle *(shan-gol)*
giungla *(shoon-glah)*

K

karate *(ka-ra-ri)*

karate *(kah-rah-teh)*

kangaroo *(ken-ghe-ru)*
canguro *(cahn-goo-roh)*

kayak *(ka-iac)*   **kayak** *(kah-ee-ahk)*

kennel *(ke-nol)*
canile *(cah-nee-leh)*

ketchup
(ket-shop)

ketchup
(keht-coop)

kettle
(ke-rol)

bollitore
(boh-lee-toh-reh)

kite
(kait)

aquilone
(ah-coo-ee-loh-neh)

key *(kii)*   **chiave** *(kee-ah-veh)*

35

K

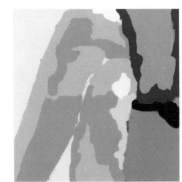

knees *(kniis)*

ginocchio *(she-noh-kee-oh)*

kitten *(ki-ren)*   **micino** *(mee-she-noh)*

knife *(knaif)*

coltello *(cohl-teh-loh)*

koala bear *(ko-a-la/ber)*

orso koala *(ohr-soh/koh-ah-lah)*

L

labyrinth *(la-ba-rint)*
labirinto *(lah-bee-reen-toh)*

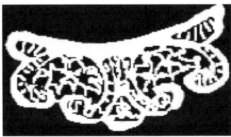

lace *(leis)*

merletto *(mehr-leh-toh)*

ladder *(la-der)*

scala *(s-cah-lah)*

ladybug *(lei-di-bog)*

coccinella *(coh-chee-neh-lah)*

L

lamb *(lamb)* agnello *(ahg-nee-eh-loh)*

lamp
(lamp)

lampada
(lahm-pah-dah)

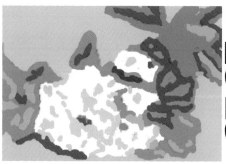

laurel
(lohu-rol)

lauro
(lah-oo-roh)

lavender
(lei-van-der)

lavanda
(lah-vahn-dah)

lawn mower
(lan-moher)

tagliaerba
(tah-glee-ah-ehr-bah)

leaf
(lif)

foglia
(foh-glee-ah)

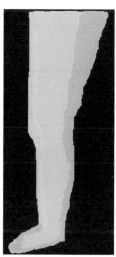

leg
(leg)

gamba
(gahm-bah)

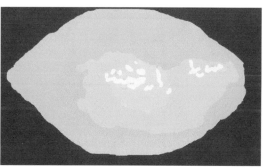

lemon
(le-mon)

limone
(lee-moh-neh)

37

L

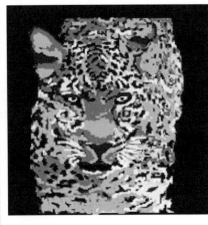

leopard
(le-perd)

leopardo
(leh-oh-pahr-doh)

lettuce
(le-rus)

lattuga
(lah-too-gah)

lightbulb
(lait-bolb)

lampadina
(lahm-pah-dee-nah)

lighthouse
(lait-jaus)

faro
(fah-roh)

lilac
(lai-lac)

lila
(lee-lah)

lime
(laim)

lime
(lee-meh)

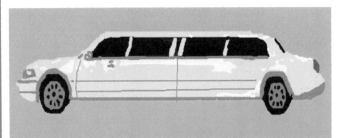

limousine *(li-mu-sin)*   limousine *(lee-moh-seen)*

lion
(la-ion)

leone
(leh-oh-neh)

38

lips
(lips)

labbra *(lah-brah)*

L

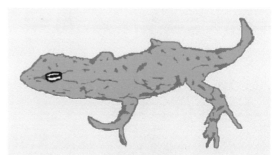

lizard *(li-zard)* **lucertola** *(loo-chehr-toh-lah)*

lobster
(lobs-ter)

astice
(ahs-tee-cheh)

lock
(lock)

serratura
(seh-rrah-too-rah)

lollipop
(lo-li-pop)

lecca-lecca
(leh-cah/leh-cah)

lovebirds
(lov-berds)

pericos
(peh-ree-cohs)

luggage *(loh-ghesh)*
bagaglio *(bah-gah-glee-oh)*

lynx
(linkz)

lince
(leen-cheh)

39

M

magazine *(ma-ga-zin)*
rivista *(ree-vees-tah)*

magician *(ma-gi-shian)*

mago *(mah-goh)*

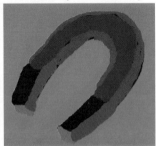

magnet *(mag-net)*

magnete *(mahg-nee-eh-teh)*

magnolia *(mag-no-li-a)*

magnolie *(mahg-noh-lee-eh)*

maid *(meid)*

cameriera *(cah-meh-ree-eh-rah)*

mailbox *(meil-box)*

cassetta postale *(cah-seh-tah/pohs-tah-le)*

mammoth *(me-moz)*
mammut *(mah-moot)*

mandarin *(men-da-rin)*
mandarino *(mahn-dah-ree-noh)*

40

M

mango *(mein-go)*
mango *(mahn-goh)*

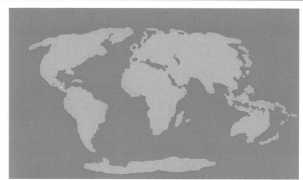

map *(map)*   **mappa** *(mah-pah)*

maple leaf *(mei-pol/lif)*
foglia dell'acero
(foh-glee-ah/dehl/ah-ceh-roh)

marigold
(me-ri-gold)

calendula
(cah-lehn-doo-lah)

mask
(mask)

maschera *(mahs-keh-rah)*

matchbox
(mhatsh-box)

scatola di fiammiferi
(s-cah-toh-lah/dee/fee-ah-mee-feh-ree)

meat *(mit)*   **carne** *(cahr-neh)*

medal
(me-dal)

medaglia
(meh-dahg-lee-ah)

41

M

melon *(me-lon)*
melone *(meh-loh-neh)*

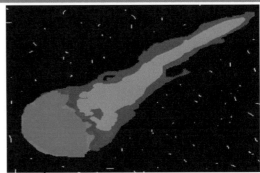

meteor *(mi-ri-or)*
meteora *(meh-tee-oh-rah)*

milk
(milk)

latte
(lah-teh)

mirror
(mi-ror)

specchio
(ehs-peh-kee-oh)

mitten
(mitn)

manopola
(mah-noh-poh-lah)

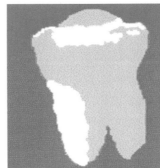

molar
(mou-ler)

molare
(moo-lah-reh)

mole *(moul)* **talpa** *(tahl-pah)*

money *(ma-ni)* **denaro** *(deh-nah-roh)*

monitor *(mo-ni-rer)*
schermo *(s-kehr-moh)*

monkey *(mon-ki)*

scimmia *(she-mee-ah)*

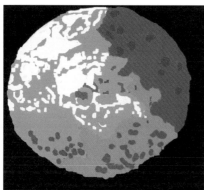

moon *(mun)*   **luna** *(loo-nah)*

mountain *(mau-ten)*
montagna *(mohn-tahg-nee-ah)*

moustache *(mos-tesh)*   **baffi** *(bah-fee)*

mouse *(maus)*   **topo** *(toh-poh)*

mushroom
(mahsh-rum)

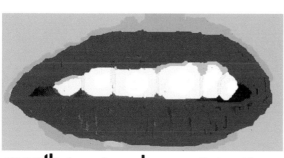

mouth *(mauz)*   **bocca** *(boh-cah)*

fungo *(foon-goh)*

N

nail
(neh-il)

unghia
(oog-nee-ah)

napkins *(nap-kins)*
tovagliolo *(toh-vah-glee-oh-loh)*

neck *(neck)*　collo *(coh-loh)*

necklace
(neck-leis)

collana
(coh-lah-nah)

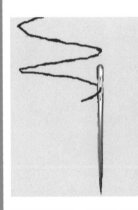

needle
(ni-rol)

ago
(ah-goh)

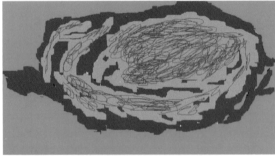

nest
(nest)

nido
(nee-doh)

newspaper *(nius-pei-per)*
giornale *(shohr-nah-leh)*

nightingale
(nai-tin-ghel)

usignolo
(oo-seeg-nee-oh-loh)

44

N

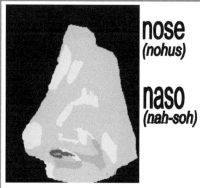

nose
(nohus)

naso
(nah-soh)

notebook *(nout-buk)*
quaderno *(coo-ah-dehr-noh)*

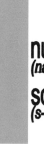

nutcracker
(nat-cra-quer)

schiaccianoci
(s-cah-chah-noh-chee)

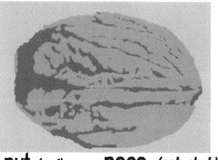

nut *(nat)*   noce *(noh-cheh)*

O

oar *(oiar)*   remo *(reh-moh)*

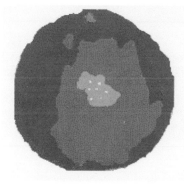

octopus *(oc-tu-pus)*
polpo *(pool-poh)*

onion
(o-ni-on)

cipolla
(she-poh-lah)

orange
(o-ransh)

arancia
(ah-rahn-shah)

O

orchid
(or-kid)

orchidea *(ohr-kee-dee-ah)*

ostrich
(os-trich)

struzzo
(s-troo-zoh)

owl
(aul)

gufo
(goo-phoh)

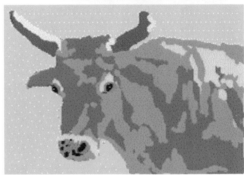

ox
(ox)

bue
(boo-eh)

P

paint
(peint)

pittura
(pee-too-rah)

palm
(palm)

palma
(pahl-mah)

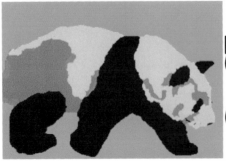

panda
(pan-da)

panda
(pahn-dah)

pansy
(pen-si)

viola del pensiero
(vee-oh-lah/dehl/pehn-see-eh-roh)

P

panther *(pan-ter)*   pantera *(pahn-teh-rah)*

parachute
(per-a-shut)

paracadute
(pah-rah-cah-doo-teh)

parakeet
(per-kit)

perico
(peh-ree-coh)

parasol
(per-a-sol)

ombrellone *(ohm-breh-loo-neh)*

parrot
(pe-rrot)

pappagallo
(pah-pah-gah-loh)

parsley
(pars-li)

prezzemolo
(preh-zeh-moh-loh)

passport
(pass-port)

passaporto
(pah-sah-pohr-toh)

peach
(pish)

pesca *(pehs-cah)*

47

P

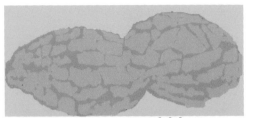

peanut *(pi-nat)* **arachide** *(ah-rah-kee-deh)*

pear
(peher)

pera
(peh-rah)

pecan
(pi-ken)

noce del Messico
(noh-cheh/dehl/meh-see-coh)

pelican
(pe-li-ken)

pellicano
(peh-lee-cah-noh)

pen
(pen)

penna
(peh-nah)

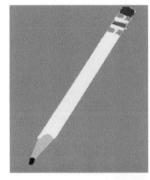

pencil
(pen-sol)

lapis
(lah-pees)

penguin
(pen-guin)

pinguino
(peeh-goo-ee-noh)

piano
(pia-no)

pianoforte *(pee-ah-noh-fohr-teh)*

P

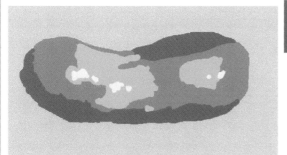

pickle *(pi-col)* sottaceto *(soh-tah-cheh-toh)*

pie *(pai)* pasticcio *(pahs-tee-choh)*

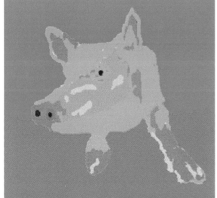

pig *(pig)* maiale *(mah-ee-ah-leh)*

pigeon *(pi-she-on)* colombo *(coh-loom-boh)*

pillow
(pi-lou)

guanciale
(goo-ahn-chah-leh)

pin
(pin)

spillo
(s-pee-loh)

pine
(pa-in)

pino
(pee-noh)

pineapple
(pa-in-a-pol)

ananas
(ah-nah-nahs)

49

P

pinecone *(pa-in-con)*

pigna *(peeg-nee-ah)*

pitcher *(pit-cer)*

brocca *(broh-cah)*

plate *(pleit)*   **piatto** *(pee-ah-toh)*

platypus *(pla-ri-pus)*
ornitorinco *(ohr-nee-toh-reen-coh)*

plum *(plam)*

prugna *(proog-nee-ah)*

polar bear *(po-lar/beher)*

orso polare *(ohr-soh/poh-lah-reh)*

pony *(po-ni)*

pony *(po-nee)*

50

pot *(pot)*   **pentola** *(peen-toh-lah)*

P

potato *(po-tei-ro)*
patata *(pah-tah-tah)*

present *(pre-sent)*
regalo *(reh-gah-loh)*

pumpkin
(pamp-kin)

zucca
(zoo-cah)

puppy
(pa-pi)

cucciolo
(coo-choh-loh)

Q

quail
(cueol)

quaglia
(coo-ahg-lee-ah)

quarter
(cuo-ra)

un quarto de dollar
(oon/coo-ahr-toh/deh/doh-llahr)

queen
(cuín)

regina *(reh-gee-nah)*

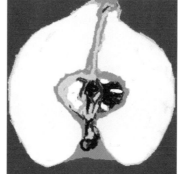

quince
(cuins)

mela cotogna
(meh-lah/coh-to-nee-ah)

51

R

raccoon *(ra-cun)*

procione *(proh-choh-neh)*

rabbit *(ra-bit)*
coniglio *(coh-neeg-lee-oh)*

racket *(ra-ket)*

racchetta *(rah-keh-tah)*

radio *(rei-dio)*

radio *(rah-dee-oh)*

rainbow *(rain-bow)*   arcobaleno *(ahr-coh-bah-leh-noh)*

radish *(ra-dish)*
ravanello *(rah-vah-neh-loh)*

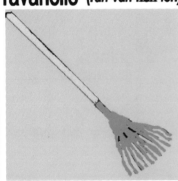

rake *(reik)*

rastrello *(rahs-treh-loh)*

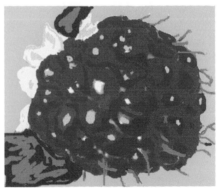

raspberry *(rasp-beh-rri)*
lampone *(lahm-poh-neh)*

R

rat *(rat)*   ratto *(rah-toh)*

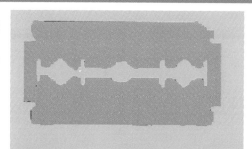

razor *(rei-zor)* rasoio *(rah-soh-ee-oh)*

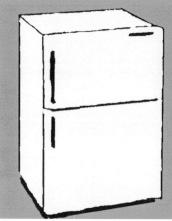

refrigerator
(re-fri-shi-rei-ror)

frigorifero
(phree-goh-ree-phe-roh)

reindeer *(rain-dier)* renna *(reh-nah)*

rhinoceros *(rai-no-ce-res)*
rinoceronte *(ree-noh-ceh-rohn-teh)*

ribbon
(ri-bon)

nastro
(nahs-troh)

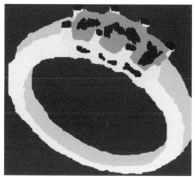

ring
(ring)

anello *(ah-neh-loh)*

robot
(ru-bot)

robot
(roh-boht)

53

R

rock *(rock)*   pietra *(pee-eh-trah)*

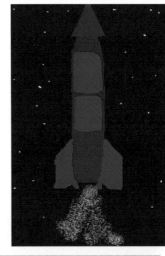

rocket *(ro-ket)*

razzo *(rah-zoh)*

roof *(ruf)*   tetto *(teh-toh)*

rooster *(rus-ter)*

gallo *(gah-loh)*

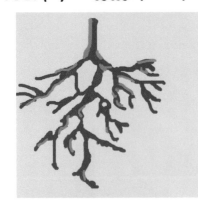

root *(rut)*

radice *(rah-dee-cheh)*

rope *(roup)*

corda *(cohr-dah)*

rose *(rous)*

rosa *(roh-sah)*

ruler *(ru-ler)*
righello *(ree-geh-loh)*

54

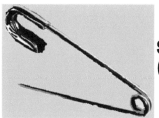

safety pin *(seif-ti-pin)*

S

salamander *(sal-a-mehn-der)*
salamandra *(sah-lah-mahn-drah)*

spilla di sicurezza
(s-pee-lah/dee/see-coo-reh-zah)

sandal *(san-dal)*
sandalo *(sahn-dah-loh)*

sausage *(so-sesh)*
salsiccia *(sahl-see-chah)*

scale *(skel)*
bilancia *(bee-lahn-shah)*

school
(scul)

scuola
(s-coo-oh-lah)

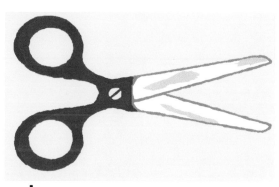

scissors *(si-sors)*
forbice *(fohr-bee-cheh)*

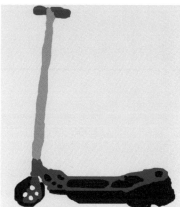

scooter
(scu-rer)

monopattino *(moh-noh-pah-tee-noh)*

55

S

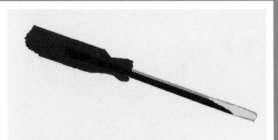

screwdriver *(scru-drai-ver)*
cacciavite *(cah-chee-ah-vee-teh)*

scorpion *(scor-pion)*
scorpione *(ehs-cohr-pee-oh-neh)*

seagull
(si-gul)

gabbiano
(gah-bee-ah-noh)

sea lion *(si/la-ion)*
otaria *(oh-tah-ree-ah)*

sheep
(shiip)

pecora
(peh-coh-rah)

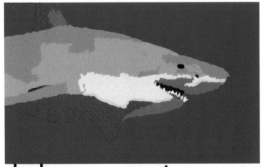

shark *(shark)*   **squalo** *(s-coo-ah-loh)*

shell
(shel)

guscio
(goo-shoh)

ship *(ship)*   **nave** *(nah-veh)*

S

shirt
(shert)

camicia
(cah-mee-chah)

shoe *(shu)*
scarpa *(s-cahr-pah)*

shorts *(shorts)*   shorts *(shorts)*

shoulder
(shoul-der)

spalla
(s-pah-llah)

shovel
(sha-vol)

pala
(pah-lah)

shower
(sha-guer)

doccia
(doo-chah)

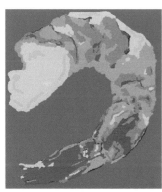

shrimp
(shrimp)

gambero
(gahm-beh-roh)

shutter
(sha-rer)

persiana
(pehr-see-ah-nah)

57

S

skillet *(s-qui-let)*   padella *(pah-deh-lah)*

skirt *(skert)*   gonna *(goh-nah)*

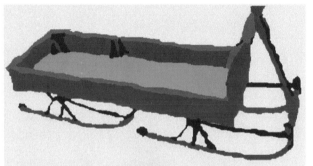

sled *(sled)*   slittino *(s-lee-tee-noh)*

snail *(s-neil)* chiocciola *(kee-oh-choh-lah)*

snake
(s-neik)

serpente *(sehr-pehn-teh)*

snow
(s-nou)

neve
(neh-veh)

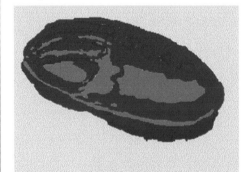

soap *(soup)*
saponetta *(sah-poh-neh-tah)*

sock
(sock)

calzino
(cahl-cee-noh))

S

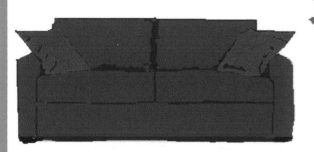

sofa *(sou-fa)*   **sofà** *(soh-phah)*

sparrow
(s-pe-rrou)

passero
(pah-seh-roh)

spider *(s-pei-der)* **ragno** *(rahg-nee-oh)*

spiderweb
(spei-der-web)

ragnatela
(rahg-nee-ah-teh-lah)

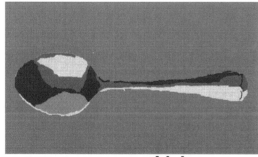

spoon *(spun)* **cucchiaio** *(coo-kee-ah-ee-oh)*

squirrel
(scuerl)

scoiattolo *(s-coh-ee-ah-toh-loh)*

stair
(ster)

scala
(s-cah-lah)

stamp
(stemp)

marca
(mahr-cah)

59

S

starfish
(star-fish)

stella di mare
(s-teh-llah/dee/mah-reh)

stork
(stork)

cicogna *(chee-goo-eh-nee-ah)*

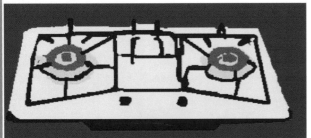

stove *(stouv)*   **cucina** *(coo-chee-nah)*

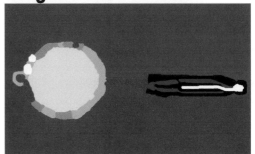

strainer *(stri-ner)*   **colino** *(coh-lee-noh)*

strawberry
(stro-beh-rri)

fragola
(phra-goh-lah)

sun
(san)

sole
(soh-leh)

sunflower
(san-fla-uer)

girasole
(she-rah-soh-leh)

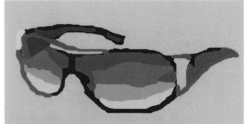

sunglasses *(san-gla-ses)*
occhiali da sole
(oh-kee-ah-leh/dah/soh-leh)

60

S

surf-board
(surf-bord)

surf-bordo
(sohrf/bohr-doh)

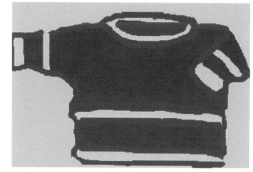

sweater *(sue-rer)*
buzo *(boo-zoh)*

T

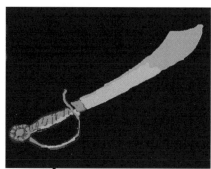

sword *(suord)*
spada *(s-pah-dah)*

table
(tei-bol)

tavolo
(tah-voh-loh)

teapot *(ti-pot)*   **teiera** *(teh-ee-eh-rah)*

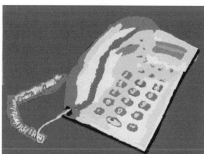

telephone
(te-le-fon)

telefono
(teh-leh-pho-noh)

telescope
(te-les-cop)

cannocchiale
(cah-noh-kee-ah-leh)

television *(te-le-vi-shion)*
televisione *(teh-leh-vee-see-oh-neh)*

61

T

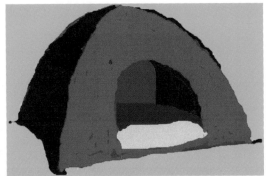

tent *(tent)* tenda *(tehn-dah)*

thumb
(zam)

pollice
(poh-lee-cheh)

tie
(tai)

cravatta
(crah-vah-tah)

tiger
(tai-gher)

tigre
(tee-greh)

toaster
(tous-ter)

tostapane
(tohs-tah-pah-neh)

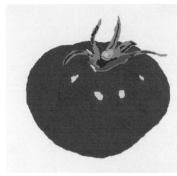

tomato
(to-mei-ro)

pomodoro
(poh-moh-doh-roh)

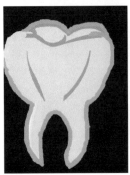

tooth
(tuz)

dente
(dehn-teh)

torch
(torsh)

torcia
(tohr-chah)

62

toucan
(tu-ken)

tucano
(too-cah-noh)

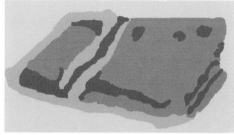

towel
(ta-uol)

asciugamano *(ah-shoo-gah-mah-noh)*

tower
(ta-wer)

torre
(toh-rreh)

train
(trein)

treno
(treh-noh)

tray *(trei)* vaschetta *(vahs-keh-tah)*

tree
(tri)

albero
(ahl-beh-roh)

truck *(track)* camion *(cah-mee-ohn)*

trumpet *(trom-pet)*
tromba *(trohm-bah)*

63

T

tulip
(tu-lip)

tulipano
(too-lee-pah-noh)

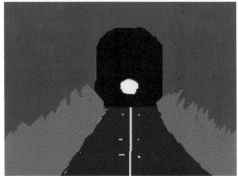

tunnel *(ta-nol)*   tunnel *(too-nehl)*

turtle
(torol)

U

tartaruga   *(tahr-tah-roo-gah)*

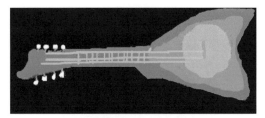

ukulele *(io-ko-le-le)*
chitarra hawaiana
(kee-tah-rrah/vah-ee-ah-nah)

umbrella
(am-bre-la)

ombrello
(ohm-breh-lloh)

uphill
(ap-jil)

in salita *(een/sah-lee-tah)*

u turn
(iu-torn)

u volgersi
(oo/vohl-shehr-see)

64

V

valve *(valv)*
valvola *(vahl-voh-lah)*

vase *(veis)*

fioriera *(fee-oh-ree-eh-rah)*

vest *(vest)*

canottiera *(cah-noh-tee-eh-rah)*

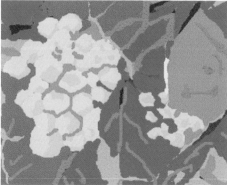

vine *(vain)*

vite *(vee-teh)*

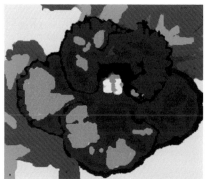

violet *(va-io-let)*

violeta *(vee-oh-leh-tah)*

violin *(va-io-lin)*

violino *(vee-oh-lee-noh)*

visor *(vai-sor)*   **visiera** *(vee-see-eh-rah)*

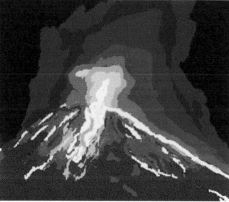

volcano *(vol-kei-no)*

vulcano *(vool-cah-noh)*

65

W

waffle *(uah-fol)*
cialda *(chah-dah)*

wagon
(uah-gon)

carro
(cah-rroh)

walkie-talkie
(ua-ki/tol-ki)

radio ricetrasmittente portatile
(rah-dee-oh/ree-chehs-trah-mee-tehn-teh/pohr-tah-tee-leh)

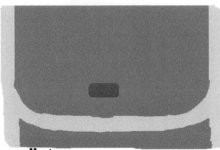

wallet *(wa-let)*
portafoglio *(pohr-tah-phoh-glee-oh)*

wasp
(uasp)

vespa
(vees-pah)

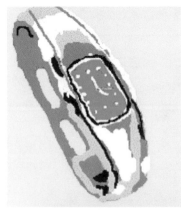

watch
(guh-atsh)

orologio
(ohr-loh-shoh)

waterfall
(ua-der-fol)

cascata
(cahs-cah-tah)

watering can *(ua-de-ring/ken)*
annaffiatoio *(ah-nah-fee-ah-toh-ee-oh)*

66

W

watermelon *(ua-der-me-lon)*
anguria *(ahn-goo-ree-ah)*

wave *(ueh-iv)*

onda *(oon-dah)*

weather vane *(ua-der/vein)*

meteo banderuola *(meh-teh-oh/bahn-deh-roh-lah)*

whale *(guel)*   **balena** *(bah-leh-nah)*

wheel *(guiol)*

ruota *(roo-oh-tah)*

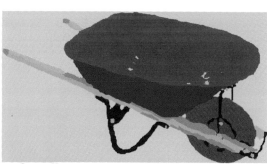

wheelbarrow *(guiol-ba-rrou)*
carriola *(cah-ree-oh-lah)*

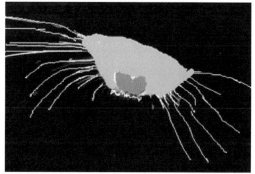

whiskers *(guis-kers)*
baffo *(bah-phoh)*

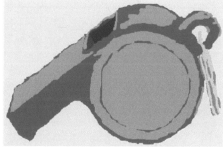

whistle *(gui-sol)*

fischietto *(fees-kee-eh-toh)*

67

W

wig *(uig)*   **parrucca** *(pah-roo-cah)*

window *(uin-dou)*

finestra *(fee-nehs-trah)*

wings *(uings)*   **ali** *(ah-lee)*

wolf *(uolf)*

lupo *(loo-poh)*

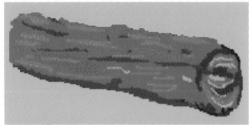

wood *(gud)*   **legno** *(lehg-nee-oh)*

wool *(gul)*

lana *(lah-nah)*

worm *(uorm)*   **verme** *(vehr-meh)*

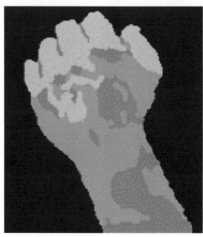

wrist *(gru-hist)*

polso *(pool-soh)*

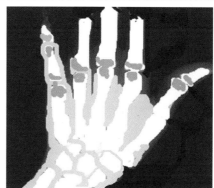

X

X- mas *(cris-mas)*

Natale *(nah-tah-leh)*

X- ray *(ex-rey)*
raggio x *(rah-shoh/eex)*

xylophone *(zai-lo-fon)*
xilófono *(xee-loh-pho-noh)*

Y

yacht *(iaht)*   **yacht** *(ee-oht)*

yam *(iam)*   **batata** *(bah-tah-tah)*

yield *(ield)*

cedere *(cheh-deh-reh)*

yogurt *(io-gurt)*

yogurt *(ee-oh-goort)*

69

Z

zebra *(zi-bra)*   **zebra** *(xzeh-brah)*

zebu *(zi-bu)*   **cebu** *(cheh-boo)*

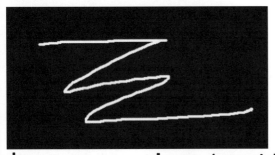

zigzag *(zig-zag)*   **zigzag** *(zeeg-zahg)*

zipper *(zi-per)*   **cerniera** *(cher-nee-eh-rah)*

A

acquaio *(ah-coo-ah-ee-oh)* faucet *(fo-set)*

acquario *(ah-coo-ah-ree-oh)* aquarium *(a-cue-rium)*

aerostato *(ah-eh-rohs-tah-toh)* balloon *(ba-lun)*

aglio *(ahg-lee-oh)* garlic *(gar-lic)*

agnello *(ahg-nee-eh-loh)* lamb *(lamb)*

ago *(ah-goh)* needle *(ni-rol)*

airplane *(er-plein)* aeroplano *(ah-eh-roh-plah-noh)*

albero *(ahl-beh-roh)* tree *(tri)*

alce *(ahl-cheh)* elk *(elk)*

ali *(ah-lee)* wings *(uings)*

amaca *(ah-mah-cah)* hammock *(ha-meck)*

ambulanza *(ahm-boo-lahn-zah)* ambulance *(am-biu-lans)*

ananas *(ah-nah-nahs)* pineapple *(pain-a-pol)*

anatra *(ah-nah-trah)* duck *(dack)*

anello *(ah-neh-loh)* ring *(ring)*

angelo *(ahn-sheh-loh)* angel *(ein-shol)*

anguilla *(ahn-goo-ee-lah)* eel *(iiol)*

anguria *(ahn-goo-ree-ah)* watermelon *(ua-der-me-lon)*

annaffiatoio *(ah-nah-fee-ah-toh-ee-oh)* watering can *(ua-de-ring/ken)*

ape *(ah-peh)* bee *(bi)*

appartamento *(ah-pahr-tah-mehn-toh)* apartment *(a-part-ment)*

aquila *(ah-coo-ee-lah)* eagle *(i-gol)*

aquilone *(ah-coo-ee-loh-neh)* kite *(kait)*

arachide *(ah-rah-kee-deh)* peanut *(pi-nat)*

arancia *(ah-rahn-shah)* orange *(o-ransh)* **arca** *(ahr-cah)* ark *(ark)*

arco *(ahr-coh)* arc *(arc)*

arcobaleno *(ahr-coh-bah-leh-noh)* rainbow *(rein-bou)*

armadietto *(ahr-mah-dee-eh-toh)* cabinet *(ca-bi-net)*

arpa *(ahr-pah)* harp *(harp)*

ascensore *(ahs-cehn-soh-reh)* elevator *(eh-leh-vei-ror)*

asciugamano *(ah-shoo-gah-mah-noh)* towel *(ta-uol)*

astice *(ahs-tee-cheh)* lobster *(lobs-ter)*

atleta *(ah-tleh-tah)* athlete *(a-tlit)*

auricolari *(ah-oo-ree-coo-lah-ree)* earphone *(iier-fon)*

autobus *(ah-oo-toh-boos)* bus *(bas)*

automobile *(ah-oo-toh-moh-bee-leh)* automobile *(au-ro-mo-bil)*

autostrada *(ah-oo-tohs-trah-dah)* highway *(hai-guei)*

autunno *(ah-oo-too-noh)* autumn *(o-rom)*

70

baffi (*bah-fee*) moustache (*mos-tesh*)

baffo (*bah-phoh*) whiskers (*guis-kers*)

bagaglio (*bah-gah-glee-oh*) luggage (*loh-ghesh*)

balena (*bah-leh-nah*) whale (*guel*)

balletto (*bah-leh-toh*) ballet (*ba-let*)

bambino (*bahm-bee-noh*) baby (*bei-bi*)

bambola (*bahm-boh-lah*) doll (*doll*)

banana (*bah-nah-nah*) banana (*ba-na-na*)

banco (*bahn-coh*) bench (*bensh*)

bandiera (*bahn-dee-eh-rah*) flag (*flahg*)

barattolo (*bah-rah-toh-loh*) can (*ken*)

bicchiere (*bee-kee-eh-reh*) goblet (*ga-blet*)

bicicletta (*bee-chee-cleh-tah*) bicycle (*bai-si-col*)

bilancia (*bee-lahn-shah*) scale (*skel*)

binocolo (*bee-noh-coh-loh*) binoculars (*bai-no-kiu-lars*)

biscotto (*bees-coh-toh*) biscuit (*bis-ket*)

bisonte (*bee-sohn-teh*) bison (*bai-son*)

bocca (*boh-cah*) mouth (*mauz*)

bocina (*boh-see-nah*) horn (*horn*)

bollitore (*boh-lee-toh-reh*) kettle (*ke-rol*)

borsetta (*bohr-seh-tah*) handbag (*hand-bag*)

bottiglia (*boh-tee-lee-ah*) bottle (*ba-rol*)

bouquet (*buh-keh*) bouquet (*buh-keh*)

braccialetto (*brah-chah-leh-toh*) bracelet (*breis-let*)

braccio (*brah-choh*) arm (*arm*)

brocca (*broh-cah*) jug (*shog*); pitcher (*pit-cer*)

broccolo (*broh-coh-loh*) broccoli (*bro-co-li*)

bruco (*broo-coh*) caterpillar (*ca-rer-pi-ler*)

bue (*boo-eh*) ox (*ox*)

burro (*boo-rroh*) butter (*ba-ter*)

busta (*boos-tah*) envelop (*en-ve-lop*)

buzo (*boo-zoh*) sweater (*sue-rer*)

cacciavite (*cah-chee-ah-vee-teh*) screwdriver (*scru-drai-ver*)

cactus (*cahc-toos*) cactus (*cac-ts*)

calendula (*cah-lehn-doo-lah*) marigold (*me-ri-gold*)

calzino (*cahl-cee-noh*) sock (*sock*)

camello (*cah-meh-loh*) camel (*ke-mol*)

cameriera (*cah-meh-ree-eh-rah*) maid (*meid*)

camicia (*cah-mee-chah*) shirt (*shert*)

camion (*cah-mee-ohn*) truck (*track*)

campana (*cahm-pah-nah*) bell (*bell*)

campo (*cahm-poh*) field (*fi-old*)

canarino (*cah-nah-ree-noh*) canary (*ke-ne-ri*)

candela (*cahn-deh-lah*) candle (*ken-dol*)

cane (*cah-neh*) dog (*dog*)

canguro (*cahn-goo-roh*) kangaroo (*ken-ghe-ru*)

canile (*cah-nee-leh*) kennel (*ke-nol*)

cannocchiale (*cah-noh-kee-ah-leh*) telescope (*te-les-cop*)

canoa (*cah-noh-ah*) canoe (*ca-nu*)

canottiera (*cah-noh-tee-eh-rah*) vest (*vest*)

cappello (*cah-peh-lloh*) hat (*hat*)

capra (*cah-prah*) goat (*gout*)

caramella alla frutta (*cah-rah-meh-lah/ah-lah/froo-tah*) jelly beans (*sheh-li/bins*)

carcere (*cahr-ceh-reh*) jail (*sheil*)

carne (*cahr-neh*) meat (*mit*)

carota (*cah-roh-tah*) carrot (*ke-rrot*)

carriola (*cah-ree-oh-lah*) wheelbarrow (*guil-ba-rrou*)

carro (*cah-rroh*) wagon (*uah-gon*)

casa (*cah-sah*) house (*haus*)

cavolo (*cah-voh-loh*) cabbage (*ca-besh*)

cascata (*cahs-cah-tah*) waterfall (*ua-der-fol*)

casco (*cahs-coh*) helmet (*hel-met*)

cassetta postale (*cah-seh-tah/pohs-tah-le*) mailbox (*meil-box*)

castello (*cahs-teh-loh*) castle (*ca-sol*)

cavalletta (*cah-vah-leh-tah*) grasshopper (*gra-sho-per*)

cavallo (*cah-vah-loh*) horse (*hors*)

cebu (*cheh-boo*) zebu (*zi-bu*)

cedere (*cheh-deh-reh*) yield (*ield*)

cerniera (*cher-nee-eh-rah*) zipper (*zi-per*)

cervo (*chehr-voh*) deer (*dii-ehr*)

cestino (*chehs-tee-noh*) basket (*bas-ket*)

cetriolo (*ceh-tree-oh-loh*) cucumber (*kiu-cum-ber*)

chiave *(kee-ah-veh)* key *(kii)*

chiesa *(quee-eh-sah)* church *(ciohrsh)*

chiocciola *(kee-oh-choh-lah)* snail *(sneil)*

chitarra *(kee-tah-rrah)* guitar *(ghi-tar)*

chitarra hawaiana *(kee-tah-rrah/vah-ee-ah-nah)* ukulele *(io-ko-le-le)*

cialda *(chah-dah)* waffle *(uah-fol)*

cicogna *(chee-goo-eh-nee-ah)* stork *(stork)*

ciliegia *(chee-lee-eh-sha)* cherry *(ce-rri)*

ciminiera *(chee-mee-nee-eh-rah)* chimney *(cim-ni)*

cintola *(seen-toh-lah)* belt *(belt)*

cioccolata *(shoh-coh-lah-tah)* chocolate *(cioh-co-leit)*

ciotola *(shoh-toh-lah)* bowl *(bo-hul)*

D

dado *(dah-doh)* dice *(dais)*

delfino *(dehl-phee-noh)* dolphin *(dol-fin)*

denaro *(deh-nah-roh)* money *(ma-ni)*

E

elefante *(eh-leh-phan-teh)*

faccia *(fah-chah)* face *(feis)*

falco *(fahl-coh)* hawk *(hak)* **falcon** *(fal-con)*

farfalla *(fahr-fah-llah)* butterfly *(ba-rer-flai)*

faro *(fah-roh)* lighthouse *(lait-jaus)*

---

cipolla *(she-poh-lah)* onion *(o-ni-on)*

circo *(sheer-coh)* circus *(sir-cus)*

clessidra *(cleh-see-drah)* hourglass *(aur-glass)*

coccinella *(coh-chee-neh-lah)* ladybug *(lei-di/bog)*

cocco *(coh-coh)* coconut *(co-co-not)*

coccodrillo *(coh-coh-dree-loh)* alligator *(a-li-ghei-ror)*

cocodrillo *(coh-coh-dree-loh)* crocodile *(cro-ca-drol)*

colino *(coh-lee-noh)* strainer *(stri-ner)*

collana *(coh-lah-nah)* necklace *(neck-leis)*

collo *(coh-loh)* neck *(neck)*

colombo *(coh-loom-boh)* pigeon *(pi-she-on)*

coltello *(cohl-teh-loh)* knife *(knaif)*

dente *(dehn-teh)* tooth *(tuz)*

dischetto *(dees-keh-toh)* disk *(disk)*

dito *(dee-toh)* finger *(fin-gher)*

doccia *(doo-chah)* shower *(sha-guer)*

dolciumi *(dool-choo-mee)* candy *(ken-di)*

eschimese *(ehs-kee-meh-seh)* eskimo *(es-ki-mo)*

fascia *(fah-shah)* bandage *(ban-dehsh)*

fata *(fah-tah)* fairy *(fe-ri)*

fazzoletto *(fah-zoh-leh-toh)* handkerchief *(hand-ker-kif)*

felce *(fehl-cheh)* fern *(fern)*

ferro di cavallo *(feh-rroh/dee/cah-vah-loh)* horseshoe *(hors-shu)*

---

coniglio *(coh-neeg-lee-oh)* rabbit *(ra-bit)*

corda *(cohr-dah)* rope *(roup)*

cornice *(cohr-nee-cheh)* frame *(freim)*

corona *(coh-roh-nah)* crown *(craun)*

cowboy *(cah-oo-boh-ee)* cowboy *(cau-boi)*

cravatta *(crah-vah-tah)* tie *(tai)*

croce *(croh-cheh)* cross *(cross)*

cubetti di ghiaccio *(coo-beh-tee/deh/gee-ah-choh)* ice cubes *(ais-kiubs)*

cucchiaio *(coo-kee-ah-ee-oh)* spoon *(spun)*

cucciolo *(coo-choh-loh)* puppy *(pa-pi)*

cucina *(coo-chee-nah)* stove *(stouv)*

culla *(coo-lah)* crib *(crib)*

cuore *(coo-oh-reh)* heart *(hart)*

domino *(doh-mee-noh)* domino *(do-mi-no)*

dottore *(doh-toh-reh)* doctor *(doc-tor)*

drago *(drah-goh)* dragon *(dra-gon)*

F

fiammingo *(fee-ah-meen-goh)* flamingo *(fla-min-go)*

fico *(fee-coh)* fig *(fig)*

fieno *(fee-eh-noh)* hay *(jey)*

finestra *(fee-nehs-trah)* window *(uin-dou)*

fiore *(fee-oh-reh)* flower *(fla-uer)*

fioriera *(fee-oh-ree-eh-rah)* vase *(veis)*

fischietto *(fees-kee-eh-toh)* whistle *(gui-sol)*

foglia (foh-glee-ah) leaf (lif)

foglia dell'acero (foh-glee-ah/dehl/ah-ceh-roh) maple leaf (mei-pol/lif)

forbice (fohr-bee-cheh) scissors (si-sors)

forchetta (fohr-cheh-tah) fork (fork)

gabbia (gah-bee-ah) cage (queich)

gabbiano (gah-bee-ah-noh) gull (goul)

gabbiano (gah-bee-ah-noh) seagull (si-gul)

galleta (gah-lleh-tah) cracker (cra-ker)

gallina (gah-lee-nah) hen (hen)

gallo (gah-loh) rooster (rus-ter)

gamba (gahm-bah) leg (leg)

gambero (gahm-beh-roh) shrimp (shrimp)

gazzella (gah-zeh-lah) gazelle (ga-zel)

gelato (sheh-lah-toh) ice cream (ais-crim)

hamburger (ahm-boor-gehr) hamburger (ham-bur-ger)

idrante (ee-drahn-teh) hydrant (hai-drant)

)igloo (ee-gloo) igloo (ai-glu)

in salita (een/sah-lee-tah) uphill (ap-jil)

incenso (een-shehn-soh) incense (in-sens)

jeans (sheens) jeans (shins)
jockey (hoh-kee) jockey (sho-ki)

---

foresta (foh-rehs-tah) forest (fo-rest)

formaggio (fohr-mah-shoh) cheese (ciss)

formica (fohr-mee-cah) ant (ant)

fragola (phra-goh-lah) strawberry (stro-beh-rri)

G

gelsomino (shehl-soh-mee-noh) jazmin (shas-min)

geranio (sheh-rah-nee-oh) geranium (sheh-re-nium)

ghepardo (geh-pahr-doh) cheetah (ci-ra)

giacchetta (shah-keh-tah) jacket (sha-ket)

giaguaro (shah-goo-ah-roh) jaguar (sha-guar)

giardino (shar-dee-noh) garden (gar-den)

ginocchio (she-noh-kee-oh) knees (kniis)

giornale (shohr-nah-leh) newspaper (nius-pei-per)

giraffa (she-rah-pha) giraffe (shi-raf)

K

karate (kah-rah-teh) karate (ka-ra-ri)
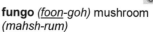

kayak (kah-ee-ahk) kayak (kah-iak)
ketchup (keht-coop) ketchup (ket-chop)

---

freccia (freh-chah) arrow (e-rrou)

frigorifero (phree-goh-ree-phe-roh) refrigerator (re-fri-shi-rei-ror)

frutta (froo-tah) fruit (frut)

fungo (foon-goh) mushroom (mahsh-rum)

fuoco (foo-oh-coh) fire (fa-ior)

girasole (she-rah-soh-leh) sunflower (san-fla-uer)

giungla (shoon-glah) jungle (shan-go)

gladiolo (glah-dee-oh-loh) gladioulus (gla-dio-los)

globo (gloh-boh) globe (glob)

gomito (goh-mee-toh) elbow (el-bou)

gonna (goh-nah) skirt (skert)

granaio (grah-nah-ee-oh) barn (barn)

granchio (grahn-kee-oh) crab (crab)

grigliata (greeh-glee-ah-tah) barbecue (bar-bi-quiu)

guanciale (goo-ahn-chah-leh) pillow (pi-lou)

guanto (goo-ahn-toh) glove (glouv)

gufo (goo-phoh) owl (aul)

L

labbra (lah-brah) lips (lips)

labirinto (lah-bee-reen-toh) labyrinth (la-ba-rint)

lampada (lahm-pah-dah) lamp (lamp)

lampadina (lahm-pah-dee-nah) lightbulb (lait-bolb)

73

lampone (*lahm-poh-neh*) raspberry (*rasp-beh-rri*)

lana (*lah-nah*) wool (*gul*)

lanterna (*lahn-tehr-nah*) flashlight (*flahsh-lait*)

lapis (*lah-pees*) pencil (*pen-sol*)

latte (*lah-teh*) milk (*milk*)

lattuga (*lah-too-gah*) lettuce (*le-rus*)

macchina fotografica (*mah-kee-nah/pho-toh-grah-phi-cah*) camera (*cah-meh-rah*)

magnete (*mahg-nee-eh-teh*) magnet (*mag-net*)

magnolie (*mahg-noh-lee-eh*) magnolia (*mag-no-lia*)

mago (*mah-goh*) magician (*ma-gi-shian*)

maiale (*mah-ee-ah-leh*) pig (*pig*)

mais (*mah-eez*) corn (*corn*)

mammut (*mah-moot*) mammoth (*me-moz*)

mandarino (*mahn-dah-ree-noh*) mandarin (*men-da-rin*)

mango (*mahn-goh*) mango (*mein-go*)

maniscalco (*mah-nees-cahl-coh*) blacksmith (*blak-smeth*)

mano (*mah-noh*) hand (*hand*)

manopola (*mah-noh-poh-lah*) mitten (*mitn*)

mappa (*mah-pah*) map (*map*)

marca (*mahr-cah*) stamp (*stemp*)

naso (*nah-soh*) nose (*nohus*)

nastro (*nahs-troh*) ribbon (*ri-bon*)

Natale (*nah-tah-leh*) X-mas (*cris-mas*)

lecca-lecca (*leh-cah/leh-cah*) lollipop (*lo-li-pop*)

leone (*leh-oh-neh*) lion (*la-ion*)

leopard (*leh-oh-pahr-doh*) leopard (*le-perd*)

lepre (*leh-preh*) hare (*her*)

letto (*leh-toh*) bed (*bed*)

libro (*lee-broh*) book (*buk*)

M

margherita (*mahr-geh-ree-tah*) daisy (*dei-si*)

marmellata (*mehr-meh-lah-tah*) jam (*sham*)

martello (*mahr-teh-loh*) hammer (*ha-mer*)

maschera (*mahs-keh-rah*) mask (*mask*)

mattoni (*mah-toh-nee*) bricks (*briks*)

medaglia (*meh-dahg-lee-ah*) medal (*me-dal*)

medusa (*meh-doo-sah*) jellyfish (*sheh-li/fish*)

mela (*meh-lah*) apple (*a-pol*)

mela cotogna (*meh-lah/coh-to-nee-ah*) quince (*cuins*)

melanzana (*meh-lahn-zah-nah*) eggplant (*egg-plant*)

melone (*meh-loh-neh*) cantaloupe (*ken-ta-lop*); melon (*me-lon*)

merletto (*mehr-leh-toh*) lace (*leis*)

N

nave (*nah-veh*) ship (*ship*)

neve (*neh-veh*) snow (*snou*)

nido (*nee-doh*) nest (*nest*)

lila (*lee-lah*) lilac (*lai-lac*)

lime (*lee-meh*) lime (*laim*)

limone (*lee-moh-neh*) lemon (*le-mon*)

limousine (*lee-moh-seen*) limousine (*li-mu-sin*)

lince (*leen-cheh*) lynx (*linkz*)

lucertola (*loo-chehr-toh-lah*) lizard (*li-zard*)

luna (*loo-nah*) moon (*mun*)

lupo (*loo-poh*) wolf (*uolf*)

meteo banderuola (*meh-teh-oh/bahn-deh-roh-lah*) weather vane (*ue-der/vein*)

meteora (*meh-tee-oh-rah*) meteor (*mi-ri-or*)

micino (*mee-she-noh*) kitten (*ki-ren*)

miele (*mee-eh-leh*) honey (*ha-ni*)

mobile (*moh-bee-leh*) furniture (*for-ni-chur*)

molare (*moo-lah-reh*) molar (*mou-ler*)

monopattino (*moh-noh-pah-tee-noh*) scooter (*s-cu-rer*)

montagna (*mohn-tahg-nee-ah*) mountain (*moun-ten*)

moquette (*moh-keht*) carpet (*car-pet*)

mora (*moh-rah*) blackberry (*blak-beh-rri*)

mosca (*mohs-cah*) fly (*flai*)

mulo (*moo-loh*) donkey (*don-ki*)

noce (*noh-cheh*) nut (*nat*)

noce del Messico (*noh-cheh/dehl/meh-see-coh*) pecan (*pi-ken*)

nuvola (*noo-voh-lah*) cloud (*claud*)

O

oca *(oh-cah)* goose *(gus)*

occhiali *(oh-kee-ah-lee)* glasses *(gla-ses)*

occhiali da sole *(oh-kee-ah-leh/dah/soh-leh)* sunglasses *(san-gla-ses)*

occhio *(oh-kee-oh)* eye *(ai)*

P

padella *(pah-deh-lah)* skillet *(ski-let)*

pagliaccio *(pahg-lee-ah-choh)* clown *(claun)*

pala *(pah-lah)* shovel *(sha-vol)*

palma *(pahl-mah)* palm *(palm)*

panda *(pahn-dah)* panda *(pan-da)*

pane *(pah-neh)* bread *(bred)*

pantera *(pahn-teh-rah)* panther *(pan-ter)*

pappagallo *(pah-pah-gah-loh)* parrot *(pe-rrot)*

paracadute *(pah-rah-cah-doo-teh)* parachute *(per-a-shut)*

parrucca *(pah-roo-cah)* wig *(uig)*

passaporto *(pah-sah-pohr-toh)* passport *(pass-port)*

passero *(pah-seh-roh)* sparrow *(spe-rrou)*

pasticcio *(pahs-tee-choh)* pie *(pai)*

patata *(pah-tah-tah)* potato *(po-tei-ro)*

pattini da ghiaccio *(pah-tee-nee/dah/gee-ah-choh)* ice skates *(ais-skeits)*

pecora *(peh-coh-rah)* sheep *(ship)*

pellicano *(peh-lee-cah-noh)* pelican *(pe-li-ken)*

---

ombrello *(ohm-breh-lloh)* umbrella *(am-bre-la)*

ombrellone *(ohm-breh-loo-neh)* parasol *(per-a-sol)*

onda *(oon-dah)* wave *(ueh-iv)*

orchidea *(ohr-kee-dee-ah)* orchid *(or-kid)*

orecchio *(oh-reh-kee-oh)* ear *(ii-er)*

ornamento *(ohr-nah-mehn-toh)* bulb *(bolb)*

---

penna *(peh-nah)* pen *(pen)*

pentola *(peen-toh-lah)* pot *(pot)*

pera *(peh-rah)* pear *(peher)*

perico *(peh-ree-coh)* parakeet *(per-kit)*

pericos *(peh-ree-cohs)* lovebirds *(lov-berds)*

persiana *(pehr-see-ah-nah)* shutter *(shu-rer)*

pesca *(pehs-cah)* peach *(pish)*

pesce *(peh-sheh)* fish *(fish)*

pettine *(peh-tee-neh)* comb *(khaomb)*

pianoforte *(pee-ah-noh-fohr-teh)* piano *(pia-no)*

piatto *(pee-ah-toh)* plate *(pleit)*

piedi *(pee-eh-dee)* feet *(fiit)*

pietra *(pee-eh-trah)* rock *(rock)*

pigna *(peeg-nee-ah)* pinecone *(pa-in-con)*

pinguino *(peen-goo-ee-noh)* penguin *(pen-guin)*

pino *(pee-noh)* pine *(pa-in)*

porcellino *(pohr-cheh-lee-noh)* hamster *(hams-ter)*

pipistrello *(pee-pee-streh-loh)* bat *(bat)*

pittura *(pee-too-rah)* paint *(peint)*

piuma *(pee-oo-mah)* feather *(feh-der)*

---

ornitorinco *(ohr-nee-toh-reen-coh)* platypus *(pla-ri-pus)*

orologio *(ohr-loh-shoh)* clock *(clock)*; watch *(uatch)*

orso *(ohr-soh)* bear *(behr)*

orso koala *(ohr-soh/koh-ah-lah)* koala bear *(koh-ah-lah/ber)*

orso polare *(ohr-soh/poh-lah-reh)* polar bear *(po-lar/beher)*

osso *(oh-soh)* bone *(boh-un)*

otaria *(oh-tah-ree-ah)* sea lion *(si/la-ion)*

---

pollo *(poo-loh)* chicken *(ci-ken)*

polpo *(pool-poh)* octopus *(oc-tu-pus)*

polso *(pool-soh)* wrist *(gru-hist)*

pomodoro *(poh-moh-doh-roh)* tomato *(to-mei-ro)*

pony *(po-nee)* pony *(po-ni)*

porcospino *(pohr-cohs-pee-noh)* hedgehog *(hedsh-jog)*

porta *(pohr-tah)* door *(dohr)*

portafoglio *(pohr-tah-phoh-glee-oh)* wallet *(ua-let)*

portone *(pohr-toh-neh)* gate *(geit)*

postoauto *(pohs-toh-ah-oo-toh)* garage *(gah-rash)*

prato *(prah-toh)* grass *(grass)*

premio *(preh-mee-oh)* award *(a-word)*

prezzemolo *(preh-zeh-moh-loh)* parsley *(pars-li)*

procione *(proh-choh-neh)* raccon *(ra-cun)*

prosciutto *(proh-shoo-toh)* ham *(ham)*

prugna *(proog-nee-ah)* plum *(plam)*

pugno *(poog-nee-oh)* fist *(fist)*

Q   **quaderno** *(coo-ah-dehr-noh)* notebook *(nout-buk)*

R   **quaglia** *(coo-ahg-lee-ah)* quail *(cuel)*

racchetta *(rah-keh-tah)* racket *(ra-ket)*

radice *(rah-dee-cheh)* root *(rut)*

radio *(rah-dee-oh)* radio *(rei-dio)*

radio ricetrasmittente portatile *(rah-dee-oh/ree-chehs-trah-mee-tehn-teh/pohr-tah-tee-leh)* walkie-talkie *(ua-ki/tol-ki)*

raggio x *(rah-shoh/eex)* X-ray *(ex-rey)*

ragnatela *(rahg-nee-ah-teh-lah)* cobweb *(cob-web)*; spiderweb *(spei-der-web)*

ragno *(rahg-nee-oh)* spider *(spei-der)*

rana *(rah-nah)* frog *(frog)*

rasoio *(rah-soh-ee-oh)* razor *(rei-zor)*

rastrello *(rahs-treh-loh)* rake *(reik)*

ratto *(rah-toh)* rat *(rat)*

ravanello *(rah-vah-neh-loh)* radish *(ra-dish)*

razzo *(rah-zoh)* rocket *(ro-ket)*

regalo *(reh-gah-loh)* gift *(gift)*

regina *(reh-gee-nah)* queen *(cuín)*

remo *(reh-moh)* oar *(oiar)*

renna *(reh-nah)* reindeer *(rein-dier)*

righello *(ree-geh-loh)* ruler *(ru-ler)*

rinoceronte *(ree-noh-ceh-rohn-teh)* rhinoceros *(rai-no-ce-res)*

rivista *(ree-vees-tah)* magazine *(ma-ga-zin)*

robot *(roh-boht)* robot *(ru-bot)*

rosa *(roh-sah)* rose *(rous)*

ruota *(roo-oh-tah)* wheel *(gui-ol)*

S

sacchetto *(sah-keh-toh)* bag *(bhag)*

salamandra *(sah-lah-mahn-drah)* salamander *(sal-a-mehn-der)*

salsiccia *(sahl-see-chah)* sausage *(so-sesh)*

sandalo *(sahn-dah-loh)* sandal *(san-dal)*

saponetta *(sah-poh-neh-tah)* soap *(soup)*

scacchi *(s-kah-kee)* chess *(cess)*

scala *(s-cah-lah)* escalator *(es-ca-leh-ii-ror)*

scala *(s-cah-lah)* ladder *(la-der)*; stair *(ster)*

scarabeo *(s-cah-rah-beh-oh)* bettle *(bi-rol)*

scarpa *(s-cahr-pah)* shoe *(shu)*

scatola di fiammiferi *(s-cah-toh-lah/dee/fee-ah-mee-feh-ree)* matchbox *(mhatsh-box)*

scatola sorpresa *(s-cah-toh-lah/sohr-preh-sah)* jack in the box *(shack/in/de/box)*

schermo *(s-kehr-moh)* monitor *(mo-ni-rer)*

schiaccianoci *(s-cah-chah-noh-chee)* nutcracker *(nat-cra-ker)*

sciacallo *(shah-cah-loh)* jackal *(sha-kol)*

scimmia *(she-mee-ah)* monkey *(mon-ki)*

scimpanzè *(sheem-pahn-zeh)* chimpanzee *(cim-pan-si)*

scoiattolo *(s-coh-ee-ah-toh-loh)* squirrel *(scuerl)*

scopa *(s-coh-pah)* broom *(brum)*

scorpione *(ehs-cohr-pee-oh-neh)* scorpion *(scor-pion)*

scrittorio *(s-cree-toh-ree-oh)* desk *(desk)*

scuola *(s-coo-oh-lah)* school *(s-cul)*

spada *(s-pah-dah)* sword spada *(suord)*

spilla di sicurezza *(s-pee-lah/dee/see-coo-reh-zah)* safety pin *(seif-ti/pin)*

spillo *(s-pee-loh)* pin *(pin)*

squalo *(s-coo-ah-loh)* shark *(shark)*

staccionata *(s-tah-choh-nah-tah)* fence *(fens)*

stella di mare *(s-teh-llah/dee/mah-reh)* starfish *(star-fish)*

stirare *(s-tee-rah-reh)* iron *(ai-ron)*

stivale *(s-tee-vah-leh)* boot *(buht)*

struzzo *(s-troo-zoh)* ostrich *(os-trich)*

succo *(soo-coh)* juice *(shuss)*

surf-bordo *(sohrf/bohr-doh)* surf-board *(sorf-bord)*

svaligiatore *(s-vah-lee-shah-toh-reh)* burglar *(behr-glehr)*

tagliaerba *(tah-glee-ah-ehr-bah)* lawn mower *(lan-moher)*

talpa *(tahl-pah)* mole *(moul)*

tamburo *(tahm-boo-roh)* drum *(drom)*

tartaruga *(tahr-tah-roo-gah)* turtle *(tor-rl)*

tavolo *(tah-voh-loh)* table *(tei-bol)*

tazza *(tah-zzah)* cup *(cap)*

teiera *(teh-ee-eh-rah)* teapot *(ti-pot)*

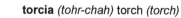

telefono *(teh-leh-pho-noh)* telephone *(te-le-fon)*

televisione *(teh-leh-vee-see-oh-neh)* television *(te-le-vi-shion)*

tenda *(tehn-dah)* tent *(tent)*

tenuta *(teh-noo-tah)* farm *(farm)*

terra *(teh-rrah)* earth *(erth)*

testa *(tehs-tah)* head *(hed)*

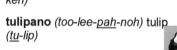

tetto *(teh-toh)* roof *(ruf)*

tigre *(tee-greh)* tiger *(tai-ger)*

topo *(toh-poh)* mouse *(maus)*

torcia *(tohr-chah)* torch *(torch)*

torre *(toh-rreh)* tower *(ta-wer)*

torta *(tohr-tah)* cake *(queik)*

tostapane *(tohs-tah-pah-neh)* toaster *(tous-ter)*

tovagliolo *(toh-vah-glee-oh-loh)* napkins *(nap-kins)*

treno *(treh-noh)* train *(trein)*

tromba *(trohm-bah)* trumpet *(trom-pet)*

tucano *(too-cah-noh)* toucan *(tu-ken)*

tulipano *(too-lee-pah-noh)* tulip *(tu-lip)*

u volgersi *(oo/vohl-shehr-see)* u-turn *(iu-tern)*

uccello *(oo-cheh-loh)* bird *(bird)*

un quarto de dollar *(oon/coo-ahr-toh/deh/doh-llahr)* quarter *(cuo-ra)*

unghia *(oog-nee-ah)* nail *(neil)*

uovo *(oo-oh-voh)* egg *(egg)*

usignolo *(oo-seeg-nee-oh-loh)* nightingale *(nai-tin-ghel)*

uva *(oo-vah)* grapes *(greips)*

vacca *(vah-cah)* cow *(cau)*

valvola *(vahl-voh-lah)* valve *(valv)*

vaschetta *(vahs-keh-tah)* tray *(trei)*

vasetto *(vah-seh-toh)* jar *(shar)*

ventilatore *(vehn-tee-lah-toh-reh)* fan *(fen)*

verme *(vehr-meh)* worm *(uorm)*

vespa *(vees-pah)* wasp *(wasp)*

vestito *(vehs-tee-toh)* dress *(dress)*

viola del pensiero *(vee-oh-lah/dehl/pehn-see-eh-roh)* pansy *(pen-si)*

violeta *(vee-oh-leh-tah)* violet *(va-io-let)*

violino *(vee-oh-lee-noh)* violin *(va-io-lin)*

visiera *(vee-see-eh-rah)* visor *(vai-sor)*

vite *(vee-teh)* vine *(vain)*

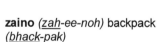

vitello *(vee-teh-loh)* calf *(calf)*

volpe *(vohl-peh)* fox *(fox)*

vulcano volcano *(vol-kei-no)*

xilófono *(xee-loh-pho-noh)* xylophone *(zai-lo-fon)*

zaino *(zah-ee-noh)* backpack *(bhack-pak)*

zappa *(zah-pah)* hoe *hou*

zebra *(xzeh-brah)* zebra *(zi-bra)*

zigzag *(zeeg-zahg)* zigzag *(zig-zag)*

zucca *(zoo-cah)* pumpkin *(pamp-kin)*

yacht *(ee-oht)* yacht *(iaht)*

yogurt *(ee-oh-goort)* yogurt *(io-gurt)*

77

THE ALPHABET
(di/al-fa-bet)

L'ALFABETO
(ehl/ahl-pha-beh-toh)

(ei)	**A**	*(a)*	*(en)*	**N**	*(eh-neh)*
(bi)	**B**	*(bee)*	*(ou)*	**O**	*(oh)*
(si)	**C**	*(chee)*	*(pi)*	**P**	*(pee)*
(di)	**D**	*(dee)*	*(chiu)*	**Q**	*(coo)*
(i)	**E**	*(eh)*	*(ar)*	**R**	*(eh-rreh)*
(ef)	**F**	*(eh-feh)*	*(as)*	**S**	*(eh-seh)*
(gi)	**G**	*(she)*	*(ti)*	**T**	*(tee)*
(eich)	**H**	*(ah-cah)*	*(iu)*	**U**	*(oo)*
(ai)	**I**	*(ee)*	*(vi)*	**V**	*(veh)*
(gei)	**J**	—	*(da-bliu)*	**W**	—
(kei)	**K**	—	*(ex)*	**X**	—
(el)	**L**	*(eh-leh)*	*(guai)*	**Y**	—
(em)	**M**	*(eh-meh)*	*(zi)*	**Z**	*(zeh-tah)*

THE COLORS
(di/co-lors)

I COLORI
(ee/coh-loh-ree)

red *(red)* — rosso *(roo-soh)*
orange *(o-ransh)* — arancione *(ah-rahn-shoh-neh)*
yellow *(ie-lou)* — giallo *(shah-lloh)*
green *(grin)* — verde *(vehr-deh)*
blue *(blu)* — blu *(bloo)*
purple *(por-pol)* — viola *(vee-oh-lah)*
pink *(pink)* — rosa *(roh-sah)*
grey *(grei)* — bigio *(bee-shoh)*
black *(black)* — nero *(neh-roh)*
white *(guait)* — bianco *(bee-ahn-coh)*

THE NUMBERS
(di/nam-bers)

I NUMERI
(ee/noo-meh-ree)

one *(uan)*	1	uno *(oo-noh)*
two *(chu)*	2	due *(doo-eh)*
three *(tri)*	3	tre *(threh)*
four *(for)*	4	quattro *(coo-ah-troh)*
five *(faiv)*	5	cinque *(sheen-coo-eh)*
six *(six)*	6	sei *(seh-ee)*
seven *(se-ven)*	7	sette *(seh-teh)*
eight *(eit)*	8	otto *(oh-toh)*
nine *(nain)*	9	nove *(noh-veh)*
ten *(ten)*	10	dieci *(dee-eh-chee)*

THE FAMILY
(di/fa-mi-li)

LA FAMIGLIA
(lah/fah-meeg-lee-ah)

father *(fa-der)* — padre *(pah-dreh)*
mother *(ma-der)* — madre *(mah-dreh)*
son *(san)* — figlio *(feeg-lee-oh)*
daughter *(do-ra)* — figlia *(feeg-lee-ah)*
brother *(bro-der)* — fratello *(frah-teh-loh)*
sister *(sis-ter)* — sorella *(soh-reh-lah)*
grandfather *(grand-fa-der)* — nonno *(noh-noh)*
grandmother *(grand-mo-der)* — nonna *(noh-nah)*
grandson *(grand-son)* — nipotino *(nee-poh-tee-noh)*
granddaughter *(grand-do-ra)* — nipote *(nee-poh-teh)*

THE DAYS OF THE WEEK
(di/deis/of-di-wik)

I GIORNI DELLA SETIMANA
(ee/shohr-nee/deh-llah/seh-tee-mah-nah)

Monday *(man-dei)*

Tuesday *(tius-dai)*

Wednesday *(wens-dai)*

Thursday *(ters-dai)*

Friday *(frai-dei)*

Saturday *(sa-rur-dai)*

Sunday *(san-dei)*

Lunedì *(loo-neh-dee)*

Martedì *(mahr-teh-dee)*

Mercoledì *(mehr-coh-leh-dee)*

Giovedì *(shoh-vehr-dee)*

Venerdì *(veh-nehr-dee)*

Sabato *(sáh-bah-toh)*

Domenica *(doh-meh-nee-cah)*

THE MONTHS OF THE YEAR
(di/monts/of/di/iar)

I MESI DELL'ANNO
(ee/meh-see/dehl/ah-noh)

January *(sha-niu-e-ri)*

February *(fe-bru-ei-ri)*

March *(march)*

April *(ei-prol)*

May *(mei)*

June *(shun)*

July *(shu-lai)*

August *(au-gost)*

September *(sep-tem-ber)*

October *(oc-toh-ber)*

November *(no-vem-ber)*

December *(di-sem-ber)*

Gennaio *(she-nah-ee-oh)*

Febbraio *(feh-brah-ee-oh)*

Marzo *(mahr-zoh)*

Aprile *(ah-pree-leh)*

Maggio *(mah-shoh)*

Giugno *(shoo-nee-oh)*

Luglio *(loog-lee-oh)*

Agosto *(ah-gohs-toh)*

Settembre *(seh-tehm-breh)*

Ottobre *(oh-too-breh)*

Novembre *(noh-vehm-breh)*

Dicembre *(dee-chehm-breh)*

THE SEASONS
(di/si-sons)

LE STAGIONI
(leh/ehs-tah-shoh-nee)

Spring *(es-pring)*

Fall *(fol)*

Summer *(sa-mer)*

Winter *(win-ter)*

Primavera *(pree-mah-veh-rah)*

Autunno *(ah-oo-too-noh)*

Estate *(ehs-tah-teh)*

Inverno *(een-vehr-noh)*

LaVergne, TN USA
18 January 2010
1676LVUK00004B